# JOURNEY

*of a*

# CONQUEROR

## JANICE CLARK HAYES

OVERCOMING ABUSE WITH FAITH AND COURAGE

WinePress Publishing (PO Box 428, Enumclaw, WA 98022) functions only as book publisher. As such, the ultimate design, content, editorial accuracy, and views expressed or implied in this work are those of the author.

Unless otherwise noted, all Scriptures are taken from the Holy Bible, *New Living Translation,* copyright © 1996, 2004 by Tyndale Charitable Trust. Used by permission of Tyndale House Publishers, Wheaton, Illinois 60189. All rights reserved.

ISBN 13: 978-1-57921-947-5
ISBN 10: 1-57921-947-0
Library of Congress Catalog Card Number: 2007943304

Printed in South Korea.

*To my mother*

# Betty Tyndall Clark

DECEMBER 10, 1927–AUGUST 29, 2007

*One of her greatest gifts to me is the inner strength
to move forward no matter what the circumstance.
She believed in me as only a mother can.*

**Thank you, Mom!**

# Contents

# Acknowledgments

How does one begin to acknowledge the incredible individuals who have influenced a life to come to this place in time to begin to serve the Lord fully and completely? I believed and lived Romans 8:28 even before I accepted the Lord Jesus Christ as my Savior and before I had begun to read the Bible for myself. When Holy Spirit was wooing me, I knew in my heart that this day would come. The individuals He placed in my life to shape and guide me along the way are far too numerous to mention, though eventually, as I write additional books, these people will come to light.

I first thank my Lord for never giving up on me, for loving me in spite of myself, and for coming after me when I was the lost sheep of His flock. I praise Him and am humbled to call myself His daughter.

Second, I want to thank my sister, Sandy Parker, who first accepted Christ and then passionately sought to introduce Him to me. Her fervent prayers, in spite of the trials and tribulations she encountered, were heard in heaven. Her witnessing to me was a powerful seed. Then she and I entered into a strong partnership that enabled us to walk together through many a fiery storm. Ultimately, that partnership was a key to our mother's salvation.

Third, I want to thank my husband, Glen Hayes, the most unexpected blessing God has ever bestowed on me. When I least anticipated it, God opened my heart and my life to a helpmate who loves Him more than anyone or anything else and then loves me second. Glen is also an anointed teacher of the Word and has thus provided to me insight I have never had before, preparing me for the ministry into which we are both walking as one.

Fourth, I want to thank my dear brothers and sisters in both North Carolina and Georgia, as well as those scattered throughout the US, who carried me throughout the early years and these later years. If I named you all, I would need another book; but you know who you are. You have mentored me, prayed for me, lifted me when the days were dark, and celebrated with me when the darkness was dispelled. Without your being "Jesus with skin on," my climb up the mountain out of the valleys would have been much lonelier.

Last and certainly not least, I would like to thank my bishop and his wife, Bishop Jim Bolin and Pastor Robin Bolin of Trinity Chapel in Powder Springs, Georgia, for providing such an honest, Christ-centered house of God. From the first moment I stepped foot into that church home, I knew God was in charge and Bishop received his authority and instruction directly from Him. I knew I was covered as well. No matter in what direction God takes my life from this point forward, it will be covered and under appropriate guidance and authority.

This book is only the beginning of stepping into the calling of my life, answering the charge that has been destined from the foundations of time. I pray that I am worthy of the mantle of responsibility for which our Lord and Creator has designed me. There are thousands of bruised hearts that I pray these pages will comfort. As I step into this ministry, I seek His wisdom and discernment, ready to serve wherever and whenever He calls.

*In Him always and in all ways,*

**JANICE CLARK HAYES**

# Introduction

y hope is that what you hold in your hands is a gift of healing, for you or someone that you love. Decades passed before I realized that I was a victim of mental, verbal, and emotional abuse. More time would pass before I would begin to understand the powerful complexities of my own circumstances, and then how I might be able to utilize that understanding to assist others in healing.

Abuse comes in so many forms that we often fail to recognize it, and then berate ourselves for allowing it to occur. This book is not about blaming an abuser, nor is it about figuring out the source or even when and how it began. It is about recognizing abuse for what it is and understanding the destructive nature of its power. This journey is about finding the path to healing and the strength to break free of its shackles.

No one can break the bondage of abuse on her or his own, no matter how strong the commitment. The abuser is an expert at isolating and eroding his or her victim. Throughout these poems, you will sense the growing presence of a support network, but more importantly, you will witness my growing reliance on my Lord.

Building faith and courage to the point that you or someone you love can walk away from the abuse will be different for each individual. In my own case, it was literally decades, but God used my weakness for His purpose: this book and my reaching out to you. He has also used it to heal my family. My former husband and our sons have healed their relationships, which was one of my prayers for them.

My most important message to you as you begin to share my journey with me is to have hope. Our Lord, Abba, our Father, *does not make junk*—my favorite phrase and the one that carried me through some of my darkest moments. He has a purpose for your life. Do not give up on yourself, for He has not given up on you. It took me thirty years to value myself and understand that *He values me!* I have spent more than twenty-seven years writing these poems and taking these photographs, and my prayer is that you will be spared some of those years.

One final thought is for the men reading this book who are victims of abuse. I have tremendous empathy for you. I cannot begin to understand how it must feel in today's society to be a male victim of an abuser. Society ridicules you for not being "macho" and "standing up for yourself," yet this same society allows abusers to stalk and murder victims. This same society for generations turned its back on what happened behind closed doors. Please understand it is the abuser who is at fault. Nothing is wrong with you. You have every right to feel violated, be protected, be removed from the situation, and be released from the fear and stress, as does any female.

I pray that sharing my journey will bring you peace and a pathway to freedom.

*I remain forever in Him always in all ways,*

**JANICE CLARK HAYES**

## PART 1

# *The Yearning*

ost people desire to be loved, to be part of something greater than themselves that gives back a sense of belonging, a sense of respect, a sense of worth. Individuals caught in abusive relationships often have a stronger need for that emotional connection. The cause is not important at this juncture, but recognizing the need is: the yearning to be loved and to be wanted.

The yearning begins to overrule caution flags that would normally arise in potentially harmful situations. The yearning also begins to distort one's sense of self-worth and one's perspective on the world. It even exaggerates the importance of others' perspectives.

What earlier in your life may have seemed like a normal future hope now seems like the impossible dream. Who you once saw in the mirror has been replaced by a stranger you no longer recognize; perhaps you barely remember the person who occupied your body what seems like a lifetime ago. All you know is there exists a tremendous emptiness inside of you that needs to be filled.

Please love me, value me, make me feel like I am worth something . . .

# Choose Me

*See me . . .*

Don't look past me or through me

Notice this person here and now

Pause to capture the essence of me

*Engage me . . .*

Delight in unraveling my mysteries

Debate me on the meaning of eternity

Dance with me under the stars

*Know me . . .*

> See beneath this exterior covering
>
> Understand the depths of my soul
>
> Believe in the value of my gifts

*Accept me . . .*

> Wrap me in your unconditional love
>
> Treat my love as a priceless jewel
>
> Be my protector and my king

*Complete me . . .*

> Make my dreams come true
>
> Be my strength when I am weak
>
> Need me as I need you

*Love me . . .*

> Open your heart totally to mine
>
> Fill my life with yours
>
> Build with me a new reality

# Waiting

Moisture gathers in the hollow of her chest

Reflections in the subtle rise and fall of each breath

Heat holds her prisoner, forbidding movement

Except for her eyes, not resting a moment

Her skin bronzes, hair reflects sun's gold

Her back glistens as the day grows old

Heat images intensify with each crawling hour

Searching eyes scan from horizon to guard tower

Evening's call vacates the beach save one
Hers the lone silhouette facing the setting sun
An occasional couple trespasses through her solitude
Nothing can pierce the darkness of her mood

The full moon rises on cue with ocean reflections
Chill of night air intensifies her emotions
Soothing sounds of ocean waves go unheard
No one to blanket her with loving words

One bright star glimmers above in the sky
An ember of hope in her heart refuses to die
"Somebody, somewhere will love me
   . . . just wait long enough to see . . . ."

# *Why Would Anyone?*

So lonely beneath the bright façade

So much energy to keep it maintained

So convincing, all believe it

So powerful, no one comes close

Why would anyone?

Why would anyone want what is on the inside?

Wanting honest love, tired of games

Wanting safe love, tired of manipulation

Wanting intimate love, tired of withdrawal

Wanting agape love, tired of selfishness


Why would anyone?

Why would anyone want to expend effort on me?


Accused of thinking too much

Accused of feeling too much

Accused of expressing too much

Accused of touching too much


Why would anyone?

Why would anyone want to tolerate me?


Change the way you dress

Change the way you speak

Change the way you self-present

Change the way you interact


Why would anyone?

Why would anyone want me the way I am?


On the inside, crying for acceptance

On the inside, needing pure love

On the inside, wanting simple assurance

On the inside, fearing rejection


Why would anyone?

Why would anyone care what's on the inside?


Better take what I can get

Better take what sounds reasonable

Better forget my heart and my instinct

Better forget myself because


Why would anyone?

Why would anyone want me?

# *Please and Peace*

To make others happy and
　　　Keep my world free from strife
Those goals superseded all others
　　　Please and Peace ruled my life

From earliest memories
　　　Conflicts sent chills down my spine
Intercessions as peacemaker
　　　Immediately coursed through my mind

A battle 'tween parents, siblings, or friends
　　　To my world posed a threat
Determined to protect delicate balances
　　　Into the middle I would step

Emotion and passion clouding vision
　　　Preventing true recognition of cause
But at smallest sudden interruption
　　　Impetus for involved parties to pause

Proactive fixing became the solution
　　　Keep lives problem free
Juggling needs with wants
　　　The mantra, the charge for me

No needy person was ever unimportant
　　　No felt pain was too small
If in some manner I could impact
　　　I would climb the highest wall

A life spent on please and peace
　　　Chasing someone else's dreams
So much time focused on others
　　　Life's reality is not what it seems

Life decisions based on please and peace
　　　To make somebody else content
Seeking to extend the truce of life
　　　Even though its weight is like hardened
　　　cement

# Standing Alone

Clusters of smiling faces, laughter muffled around me
A relaxed touch here, a soft one-arm hug there,
Little groups contentedly inhaling and
          exhaling each other
No place open to slip into, no welcome break in a chain

I am standing alone again.

Slight shift, gentle engagement with a colleague
A bright spot, a hope for needed connection,
Words of commonality bring a spark of recognition
Light of hope extinguished as excuses are made.

I am standing alone again.

Search for familiar face, inner sigh for invitation
But pioneer must step out again, bravely seeking
Another exchange, another spark, another chance
But no, hopes dashed, different music—same dance.

I am standing alone again.

Crowded room, sparsely filled, no matter
Booming bass, rasping microphone,
          or ear-splitting applause
Total silence, all noise, just whispers
Nothing penetrates the isolation

I am standing alone again.

Quarantined, ostracized, shunned
Lord, there must be a reason.
Explain to me, help me understand, show me
This transparent tube surrounding me, keeping me
forever,

Standing alone.

*For if you return to the LORD, your relatives and your children will be treated mercifully by their captors, and they will be able to return to this land. For the LORD your God is gracious and merciful. If you return to him, he will not continue to turn his face from you.*
**(2 Chron. 30:9)**

# *The Yearning*

## MY JOURNEY

More than thirty years ago during my final college years, I did not understand that my Lord desired a personal relationship with me, Janice. I did not have a glimmer of awareness that He could satisfy the longing I felt so desperately. I only knew of the void in my life, the vacuum that sucked my self-esteem into some dark hole from which I could never retrieve it. While in this dark vortex, I began making decisions that started me down a road deeply rutted with reinforcing negative messages.

I entered into relationships that devalued me, despite the wise counsel of caring friends who could see my destructive behavior even though I could not. It was as if I were two different people. One was the excellent college student, soon to be career woman; while the other was this dark shadow who disregarded her value as a human being. The final straw was an unexpected pregnancy.

When I was already struggling with perfection in an imperfect world, I made the tragic decision to abort my child. I was blinded by the fear that I would be unacceptable, unworthy and imperfect beyond correction: pregnant as a pending honors graduate with a job awaiting me with a prominent international corporation. I felt trapped with no choice. Who would ever want me this way? Who would believe that I was still capable, intelligent, deserving of a place in society? My response to myself was no one. The father served as a chauffeur to the abortion clinic and then dropped me at my apartment afterward. That night was the first of thousands in which I struggled alone with my total unworthiness.

That was Good Friday. On Easter Sunday I went to Mass. I was raised Roman Catholic and believed in a forgiving God. After receiving Holy Communion, I felt the Lord's forgiveness wash over me in its magnificence. I experienced total solitude with Him in the church as He told me He understood my decision and forgave me. But I did not embrace His forgiveness. That Good Friday began my personal crucifixion as I hung myself on a cross for killing my child. How little I understood what had happened, either from the Lord's perspective or from mine.

The Lord persisted for thirty years until I finally comprehended the message He had been trying to communicate to me from the beginning: He gave me that child to tell me I was worthy and did have value. He does not give life lightly. He was asking me to come to Him. He was telling me that He loves me, that He is gracious and merciful and will not turn His face away from me. The first part of the verse He chose for this chapter references the children. The Lord is telling me with gentle hindsight that He showed tremendous compassion to my unborn child and would have assured mercy in this world. But I did not listen then. I did not realize He was calling me, and would not realize it for a long, long time.

Instead I stayed desperate, stuck in a vortex of needing to be valued by somebody. I sentenced myself to a life of exerting more energy than I thought possible trying to earn someone's love, trying to make the world perfect for someone so that he would not stop loving me. My heart ached to be filled, but I was going to the wrong source to fill it. Consequently my self-esteem, despite all of my efforts, kept disappearing into the dark vortex. To the world I seemed self-assured, successful, and happy. In reality I was lonely, isolated, and full of self-doubt.

# PART 2

# The Rejection

Committed to a relationship no matter what is the course often chosen by individuals who have yearned so deeply to be loved. Even when the relationship is destructive, it is still a relationship, and somehow deeply embedded in our minds is the belief that if we love enough, we can fix it.

For each of us, this is such a personal aspect of the abuse. The rejection is perceived as an absolute failure to fulfill the expectation of who we are supposed to be in the eyes of the abuser. We become owners of every rejection and allow each assault to further destroy us. Yet still we fight the good fight to make amends, because we are constantly reminded that this is "your fault."

Sadly, though, no effort—however great—will end the hurt, the isolation, the control, or the exhaustion. Years can go by before you or I even recognize that we are being abused because we are so busy trying to fix this crushed crystal of a dream.

Therein is the greatest sadness for many of us. We are so busy repairing what cannot be fixed by us that we fail to take care of us. Fixing everyone else's world to prevent emotional volcanoes from erupting dominates every waking minute and sleepless night. Depression takes hold, despair around the corner. Those are two emotional states that no one can handle alone, especially when you believe that you are not worth fixing. You must reach out and seek support from safe and trusting sources—and please seek our Lord, for He is the only one who can truly mend the great hurts within you.

# The Gatekeeper

Imperceptible at first
    Gate hidden, far away
Life with him still new
    Actions changing every day

Silently, inch at a time
    Relinquishing to him control
Decision by decision
    Blind to its toll

Socializing with his friends
    Losing touch with hers
Feeling like his pet
    Getting touched only when she deserves

Despite great feats of hospitality
    Her endless efforts to please
No return invites come to them
    Why are all so ill at ease?

Oblivious to the encircling fence
        Tighter around her each year
Now with babies inside the corral
        Urging them "go outside" without fear

Her attempt to wander near the gate
        Met with a shocking jolt
Lasso yanking her from friends
        Accusations of misconduct a lightning bolt

Bewilderment at her captivity
        Lost inside the narrow confines
Sad gazes from outside grow distant
        Her worthlessness taking root in her mind

Exquisite creature behind the iron enclosure
        Exists for his delight and pleasure
His choice to unlock the gate
        Allowing her freedom only to his measure

# Silence

Skimming the waves together, carefree
Emotions light wind easing us along
Gentle banter soft lapping waves on the bow
Joy peeking through the clouds
Respite in the rough seas past

Without warning days pass with no words
Windless sea stalling movement
Motionless in death grip of blue-green mirror
Mist thickening about us closing in
No storm, a choking void in its place

Absence of sound accentuating depth of fog
Clutching handfuls of moisture, chilling isolation
Blindly taking a step on unseen deck, fearful
Danger abounds in all directions, paralyzing
My mind reels, potential scenarios haunting

What corner, what rail, wherever are you?

    Death traps await between us

    Coiled rope to snare my foot

    Extended beam to take me down

Would you even save me from a soggy grave?

You are silent—I am lost

    Impossible to navigate without direction

    Foolish to attempt to sail alone

    Frozen by fear of movement

Doomed to drift until hull crashes on rocky shore

Or drift endlessly, hopelessly, in thick, obscure silence.

# The Battle Wall

The stones tucked tightly one upon the other
Wall of strength no one can bother
High and deep
Distance it keeps
Between you and me, your lover

Each stone carefully selected, strategically placed
Its meaning, its purpose difficult to trace
Always adding a new
Hides you from my view
As I search for answers on your face

Momentarily stones tumble, creating a break
Surging forward desperately, the chance I take
Pulling stones down
Till I see your frown
Brokenhearted, a sad retreat I make

Methodically, purposefully, the wall you rebuild
With sheer determination and strength of will
Larger, heavier stones
They'll keep you alone
Love, craving connection, shivers in the chill.

# One Last Night

Lightning makes mirrors of rooftop puddles
  Cars dash between raindrops
  Headlights make slick streets shiny
  Umbrellas hurry to dry warmth

Lighted windows, like eyes, beckon
  Each calling through the darkness
  Come, don't abandon me
  But late is the hour, stark the night

Sad faces, searching eyes
  Gazing out of glass walls tonight
  Steady rhythm of rain, haunting
  Echoing in the hollowness of aching hearts

Trapped by steel and glass, prisoner of loneliness
  Thunder ominously intensifies the emptiness
  Despair creeps steadily upward
  Filling the vacuum left by isolation

One last cry out for fulfillment
  One last grasp for a lifeline
  One last tear shed for if-onlys
  One last breath succumbing
    to darkness

# Beaten

Some days it's just too hard, too unbearable
   Too hard to sustain the delicate balance
   Too hard to keep the smile pasted on
   Too hard to pretend normal existence
   Too hard to keep climbing the cliff
      during the rockslide

I am so tired and so beaten
   No relief from the unending flood of tears
   No healing of the growing open wounds
   No unbruised skin, only more raw flesh
   No numbness to protect me from
      the searing pain

The fragile spirit is willfully crushed anew
   Each time I think there is nothing
      left to destroy
   Each time I am shocked by my naiveté
   Each time a tiny surviving piece is obliterated
   Each time the agony is a fresh assault

Death would be easier than this living
   Finally the stabbing attacks would cease
   Finally I would be invulnerable
      to the onslaught
   Finally eternal peace would be mine
   Finally I would be untouchable forever

*I go east, but he is not there. I go west, but I cannot find him. I
do not see him in the north, for he is hidden.
I look to the south, but he is concealed.*

**(Job 23:8–9)**

# The Rejection

## MY JOURNEY

As a newlywed, I could not figure out what I was doing wrong. How could I feel so lonely, so isolated, so unwanted? What did I need to change? What did I need to start doing or stop doing? I felt like a small puppy waiting desperately at its master's feet, eagerly anticipating that little pat on the head that said, "I see you there." I kept hoping that if I tried harder, loved more, was less of "me" and more of his vision of me that somehow that would be the magic answer.

But there were no magic answers, only more questions. Then I slowly stopped asking questions and retreated into myself, deciding that who I was, really was, no longer mattered. I simply worked on fulfilling the expectations of those with the most control over the peace and calm in my life. The cocoon of survival slowly began wrapping around me and would prevent any semblance of the real woman from emerging. I became a master at "eggshell walking," anticipating every conversation before it happened to soften any repercussions and prevent any volcanoes from exploding and any ice storms from freezing everything in their path.

When the Lord blessed me with my sons, I did not realize that this was His persistence in communicating to me His message of my value and worth to Him that began with my unborn child. However, I did know unequivocally that each child was a gift from the Lord, and I devoted myself to giving them all the love that had been rejected. I wanted them to know they were each valued and loved without question, without conditions, in spite of the mixed messages they were getting from their father. He deeply loved them, but without help could not stop himself from the confusing behavior that tore their worlds apart at times.

During my children's early years, my own depression and "double life" was taking its toll. I lived one life as mother extraordinaire, active community volunteer, part-time home business entrepreneur, exercise instructor, and so forth. Yet, just as in college, that was the outer shell, the cocoon. Now, however, the dark shadow had evolved into a deep darkness that threatened to consume me from within. No one knew—not even my own family—except the Lord, who kept calling my name. Finally, I began to hear it, a whisper at first. On October 10, 1989, though, His voice became clear, and I ran to Him, accepting Him as my personal Savior and submitting forever to His authority over my life. The one thing that I failed to do, however, was let Him take me down from the personal cross on which I had hung myself for killing my child. Deep within, I had yet to forgive myself for that wrong.

I sought Him and hungrily studied His Word under new church mentors. These habits—and giving Him control of my life—brought me a peace I had never known. Sadly, I did not understand fully the significance of His sacrifice for me. I still did not understand that He valued me as a person. I knew He was there for me, that He was watching over me. I knew He had been persistent enough to send me daily signs for a week to ensure that I heard Him call my name, but I still saw myself as a sinner and not as His child whom He dearly loved and wanted to bless in abundance.

So I persevered. I loved my children, loved my husband, and did the best I could to be the wife I had committed to be. I was sure God had a purpose somewhere in all of this for His will. I just did not have a clue what it was and felt that I needed to just continue on my current path. I did not know any other way.

# PART 3

# The Awareness

Slowly, you become aware of what the rejection is doing to you. Gradually, you see its different faces. You begin to understand that this enemy you have been battling all this time is not within you, but outside you. The more you understand, the more you have the strength to stand and not surrender to it.

But there's more. People beyond the tight circle created by your abuser *do love you*. They are very eager to support you and listen. They have been waiting for you to allow them into your own private circle. Out of respect, they have not interfered, but for a very long time, they have worried and prayed.

There is still more. God is there and always has been. He is waiting for you, as well, to help you gain an understanding of your value and self-worth, and to see the situation for what it really is. *He loves you and always has*. You are a chosen child of His for whom He has plans. As hard as it is to believe right now, He is watching over you and loving you. He wants you to believe that and love yourself, not for anything you do but because He made you and loves you.

Now is the time to really open your eyes and maybe for the first time ever to acknowledge what has been happening *to you* and say *enough!* I do not deserve to be treated this way—no one does.

# Erosion

Beach of pearls stretching expansively
    greeting gentle ebbing waves
Expectantly awaiting future joys
    totally innocent to dangers ahead

Wave of destruction out of nowhere
    Sarcasm . . .
In front of others, in front of her
    "All in fun," the wave said in passing.

Erosion . . .
    the wave taking some of her with him.

Another wave strikes
    Criticism . . .
Correction on how it should be done
    "You disappointed me," the wave
    said in passing.

Erosion . . .
    the wave taking more of her with him.

More waves assault
Withdrawal . . .
No touch or words of love for her
"I don't want you now," the wave
said in passing.

Erosion . . .
the wave taking still more of her with him.

Storm waves not abating
Her motherhood . . .
Placing their children in the undertow
"You don't back me up," the wave
said in passing.

Erosion . . .
the wave takes the last of her pearly
top sand with him.

Tidal wave powers in

      Selfishness . . .

Focusing on the wrong priorities—not his

      "How dare you put God first," the wave

      said in passing.


Erosion . . .

      the wave starts taking her foundation with him.


Truckloads of sand rumble in

      Friends . . .

Work, church, volunteer connections securing dunes

      "It won't last," the wave said in passing.


Erosion . . .

      the wave still drags a little of her with him.


Crafted reefs and shelf barriers arise

      Faith . . .

Courage, self-confidence, self-worth as anchors

      "I will strike again," the wave said, rising up.


Erosion . . .

      No more.

      The wave will not reach the beach.

# Can It End?

A precious tear escapes the toddler's brimming eyes
    Can't grasp Daddy's anger but can his rejection
The first of many fractures in that tender heart

    Mommy's whispers soothe
    Mommy's hugs reassure
    But what Daddy cracked, Mommy can't mend

The sting of the hit muffled by padding of diaper
    Accompanying words uncalled-for
    condemnation
The first seeds of self-doubt in an undeveloped ego

    Mommy's encouragement helps
    Mommy's presence bolsters
    But what Daddy planted, Mommy can't uproot

The handgrip on his arm demarcation of control
    Fear precluding all reactions, exception
    submission
The first flicker of escape fluttering through his mind

Mommy's shelter protects . . . sometimes
Mommy's pleas unheard . . . other times
For when Daddy demands,
Mommy is powerless

Heights equaling out, a forceful slam against a wall
Anger flashing in Son's eyes but lips
sealed shut
Violent revenge taking deep root next to escape plans

Mommy's attempts to explain, unheard
Mommy's desire to restore, lost in the storm
For the destruction Daddy has wrought is total

Then the future emerged . . .
Mommy saw Son become "Daddy"
Daughter-in-law become "Mommy"
and Grandson become "Son"

And Mommy said, "It shall end here."
No guarantees, roots are still roots
But space now exists for joy without limitation
Mistakes without condemnation
Appreciation for unconditional love

Daddy's relationship in a different dimension
Safer, distanced, rebuilding
Authority gone, someday maybe
room for healing

Sons, what powerful survivors!

The question remains to be answered:
Will Sons become "Daddy"
Or "Father"?

# Her Path

She believed.
In her heart of hearts, she blindly trusted his lead.
Even when what he told her hurt, she believed.

But she couldn't see.
With all of her wisdom, with him she was still naïve.
While he was isolating her from the world, she couldn't see.

Still she owned it.
With every breath, she felt it in her inner core.
He said it was all her fault, and she owned it.

So she reached out.
Wanting desperately to change it, repeatedly she begged him.
Unwaveringly he withdrew from her, but she reached out.

Then she sought God.
Desperate to be loved, she cried out to Him.
Wanting the blackness and emptiness to end, she sought God.

She found unconditional love.

With the Creator of everything, she rested in His acceptance.

Opening herself totally, forsaking all, she found

        unconditional love.


She discovered inner courage.

With the Healer's nurturing, she yielded unfathomable depth.

Steadily, boldly, profoundly, she discovered inner courage.


She stood apart.

Tentatively, then confidently, she stepped away

        from the control.

God within, for the first time in her life, she stood apart.


And she dazzled all with His brilliance.

# Parched

Had the pressure always been present?

Had the imbalance always been there?

Rob Peter

Pay Paul

A few more hours here

A few less hours there

Got to meet everyone's needs

Got to exceed everyone's expectations


Had the dry well always been present?

Had the inner thirst always been there?

Go longer

Cover more

A little less sleep this night

A little less food this day

Got to meet everyone's needs

Got to exceed everyone's expectations

Had the drillers always been present?

Had her naïveté always been there?

 Try harder

 Ignore the drilling

 Focus more on others this time

 More focused effort this round

Got to meet everyone's needs

Got to exceed everyone's expectations


Had the heat always been so strong?

Had the need driven her life all along?

 Bury deeper

 Strive further

 Forget self within

 Attend to those outside

Got to meet everyone's needs

Got to exceed everyone's expectations


Why now has the drilling suddenly stopped?

Why now do heat, water surge upward?

 One thought—release

 One goal—freedom

 Rush through dark self-doubt

 Cut byways of confidence

Got to meet whose needs?

Got to exceed whose expectations?


What triggers the sudden explosion?

What alters the delicate pressure?

 Drench parched ground

 Flood cracked creek beds

 Celebrate the birth of the whole person

 Empower one's gift to others

Got to meet only His needs

Got to exceed only His expectations


For when the inward is fully released outward,

One becomes accessible to God.

# White Water

White froth sprays all around me
Everywhere I look rocks abound
The angry river tosses the raft carelessly
As I search in vain to escape to higher ground

The paddle, useless, I fight to stay afloat
Fearful of falling victim to the current
Surging rapids, pummeling me, seem to gloat
As I fall into despair o'er my predicament

Why, God, must I fight to stay alive?
Where are the peaceful waters of my life?
Have I not followed You? Didn't I always strive?
Your answer was days and nights filled with strife.

Desperately I cling to the ropes of the raft
The paddle long since lost to my captor
Just staying tucked within has become a craft
Needing super strength not to succumb to
the predator

Amid the roar of the water crashing on the rocks
Your voice pierced the din, penetrating
my heart
Your perfect love reached deep down to the fear locks
Releasing my spirit, gently, as if an art

Skimming the rapids, moving swiftly downstream
Bypassing huge boulders threatening death
Suddenly life seems surreal, being awake in a dream
Growing calm overcomes me with each
shallow breath

Rocks and rapids ahead as far as I can see
My raft still thrashes and crashes as I cling
No hope of calm, no hint of reprieve
Yet inner strength to the surface, God brings

Trust me, He says, I am your protection

        I will not let you capsize, not let you drown

You, my child, are growing in My perfection

        You are headed for peace, you are homeward bound


Assured of my safety, secure in His love

        I hang on for the ride, even breaking a smile

With God as my captain, navigating from above

        I travel closer to Him with each passing mile


While the river appears the enemy, it's really just life

        The rocks and current, the choices others make

My raft, buoyed by God's love, overcomes strife

        My destination, my journey to God is straight

*Our children will also serve him.*
*Future generations will hear about the*
*wonders of the Lord.*
**(Ps. 22:30)**

# *The Awareness*

## MY JOURNEY

My own awareness came in stages. It began with my twenty-fifth wedding anniversary. I looked at myself and my life with sudden clarity. With poignancy and determination, I realized that I could not live another twenty-five years in this same manner, being what someone else wanted me to be and never exploring who I was and pursuing my life's purpose. I had yet to recognize I was a victim of abuse.

My initial discussions with my husband were well received. However, the more I began to grow and blossom, the more intense the negative behaviors became on his part. In January of 2001, I read Danielle Steele's *Journey*, a novel in which the lead character is a victim of verbal, emotional, and mental abuse. I felt as if I were standing stripped naked before the world. I came face to face with the stark reality that all the excuses I had been making for the past twenty-five years were exactly that—excuses. I was a victim of abuse.

How do I describe the emotions that swept over me in the days, weeks, and months that followed? Anger that someone as intelligent, well-educated, and knowledgeable about social welfare was herself a victim. Disgust that I was so weak that I had never stood up to him and stopped it. Disbelief that I had exposed my precious sons to this all of their lives and never stopped it.

Sudden exhaustion because I had been keeping this front up for so long—and to what end? Confusion in not knowing what I was going to do with this realization. Isolation and depression such as I had never felt before—had everyone realized this situation and just pitied me, not wanting to interfere with my choice of so long ago?

The anger reached a point at home where I insisted on counseling and anger management or I was leaving and taking our sons with me. We proceeded with the counseling, but it was superficial. The changes were temporary, and within months, the behavior returned with a vengeance. I used my writing, both the poetry and journaling, as a release. I knew God had instilled in me something worthy, a seed He wanted to use. Efforts I had made to serve Him in the past had often been met with significant resistance. I knew that was wrong; it should have been a signal to me that there was a high level of dissonance in my life. But I wasn't hearing God's message concerning my worth. I was hearing the message communicated by my husband about my lack of worth.

Soon it became clear to me that the next generation was being greatly impacted. My sons were not receiving positive modeling they needed to become healthy life mates for their future wives, nor grace-filled fathers for their future children. At this point in their lives, their relationships with their father were severely strained. The Lord was making me painfully aware of my responsibility to break the cycle, one that preceded this generation. No longer was this about my own pain, my own depression; it had become about my sons.

Somehow through the years, I had thought I was shielding them from the abuse, but the Lord revealed to me that was impossible. With terrifying simplicity, He showed me how the present was evolving rapidly into the future. Anger, hatred, and eventually violence would dominate our lives. How had my life come to this? It did not matter any longer. I only knew that it must stop, and we all deserved an opportunity to find a different way to live.

# PART 4

## The Hope

ou have made the courageous step forward to leave an abusive relationship, but now what? You are not sure you even know who you are alone. You have never defined yourself without using someone else as the other half of you, or accepting another person's evaluation of who you are. Now what? Remember, *God does not make junk!*

Now is the time to begin the exploration process under His loving care. All kinds of feelings will emerge that you have never allowed yourself the privilege of experiencing before. Instead, you listened to someone else, allowing that person to dictate what you could and could not feel.

There is no time frame for discovery. Your journey is based on trusting the Father, who created you to

reveal His purpose in you. Deal with and heal the wounds you have experienced, but don't linger there. He has far too much in store for you that is awesome and wonderful. This is a period of hope for you. Hope in the future, hope for joy, hope for peace, hope for long-needed rest.

This is not a time to look for other relationships; let our Lord be your relationship for the time being. He will not let you down, and spending time in His presence will bring healing to your wounded spirit. He will comfort you and love you.

The journey may be rough at times because you'll be traveling through new territory. But don't give up! This path is so much better than the one you traveled in the past! This one leads to life!

# Self

Our yesterdays are like the surf

      Sometimes calm, low waves

            Rolling in gently, playfully, dancing, to the sand

      Other times angry, storm-tossed seas

            Pounding the beach, churning sand and shells in the wake

      Yet always moving, always present

            Ocean to wave to beach to ocean

Our yesterdays—always new, evolving in the surf

Surviving the yesterdays, surviving the surf is

    Self—fragile, precious treasure from the sea

        Arriving on the beach, brought by the waves, intact,

        As if gently laid there by loving hands

    Self—iridescent, reflecting brilliant sun's rays from its pearl face

    Self—so delicate in its translucent beauty

    Self—so strong in the pummeling waves


Choice—do I gently lift Self from the dangers of the beach

        Caressingly brushing sand from its face?

    Do I leave it to chance confrontation

        With the bare feet and dune buggies of tomorrow?


Choose to cherish Self

    Allow it to glimmer in the brilliance of life

    Tilt it into the sun

    Study its awesome depths of beauty

    Share its jeweled loveliness with others

    Together caress it

    Grow ever more familiar with its variations and textures

    Treasure it


For Self has been created by God out of Love

# Cycle

Foreboding clouds drag overhead
    With the chill of the last battle still clinging
Evergreens stretch numbed limbs
A hushed flow of thawing trickles
    Tracking across a stern, stone face

Through masses of gray, the golden globe winks
    Heralding the reawakening
A yawning earth responds, releasing the captive spirit
The trickle gains momentum
    Tumbling aimlessly over dull, cold rock

Ever deepening pool of spring's essence sparkles

        Hinting of treasures to come

Warmth creeps imperceptibly over the dampness

The captor clutches stubbornly the winter vestige

        As the frozen cap shifts, cracks, begins the slide


Suddenly free, racing down a twinkling countenance

        A thousand diamonds now gleam

Basking in the warmth and comfort from above

Brilliant release now signaling the rebirth

        With the symphony of celebration accompanying it


Exquisite beauty of the reawakening

        Stunning all who venture near

Consuming each witness in the wake of its passion

Rendering formidable opponents powerless

        As the spirit fully embraces life

# Anger Storm

The storm rages, encompassing horizon to horizon

Winds whip the waves with fury

Pellets of water beat into submission everything alive

Darkness engulfs, isolating each being, imprisoning

*It fits . . .*

Inside me, an even greater storm rages

My anger churns my emotions constantly

My anguish batters my soul with hopelessness

Despair sucks my energy like a vacuum

*It suits . . .*

The floodwaters surge, destroying all in their path
>Projectiles strike down surprised victims
>Electricity interrupted, systems fall into total
>>disarray
>The world once recognizable now alien territory

*It matches . . .*

God's "plan" has decimated my once-certain life
>This enemy attacked my loved ones,
>>caught unaware
>My unending prayers went unheeded
>>into emptiness
>My known world trashed beyond recognition

*It hurts . . .*

The winds cease rearranging the world
>The deluge from the sky tapers to mist
>But the floodwaters remain, the stench growing
>Debris heaps everywhere, nowhere to go

*It's unbearable . . .*

Time is passing, but my life's destruction remains
>Loneliness threatens to drown me daily
>Unanswered prayers, unanswered
>>questions rot inside
>My faith lies in shambles at my feet

*It's lethal . . .*

Imperceptibly the waters recede, cleanup begins
>New homes arise on old foundations
>New friendships evolve from volunteer projects
>New lives grow from unexpected opportunities

*It's paradoxical . . .*

The anger is my only familiar territory
>My only friend in this strange land of isolation
>I see no beginnings, only endings
>I experience no opportunities, only dashed dreams

*It's desolate . . .*

The rebirthing of a community labors on
>The remnants of devastation grow fewer
>Subtle signs of prosperity decorate the landscape
>Bright paint, shiny windows, fresh flowers abound

*It's encouraging . . .*

Why such reluctance to leave this ruin of anger
>Clinging to the vestige of what was
>Fearful to embrace what is yet to be
>Not knowing how to let go of lost dreams

*It's frightening . . .*

New fields are sown, richer with transported soil
>New businesses spring from unmet demands
>New classrooms furnished with updated texts
>New equipment graces production floors

*It's miraculous . . .*

Stepping out of the shadows, I encounter the light
>Focusing, I begin to see a fresh reality
>The direct consequences of my personal tragedy
>The incredible that could not have
>>happened otherwise

*It's stunning . . .*

I need wisdom to see the blessings in this
I need faith to accept God's will in my world
I need grace to release the anger
I need God's love to greet tomorrow
It's life.

# Blooms Anew

Brilliant blossom bursts from the cactus
   Army of spines fiercely protecting its beauty
Nothing can bruise the delicate petals
Nothing can alter the breathtaking design
Some dare to reach in to no avail
   Wanting to pluck the rare bloom
Ignorant of the inner connection
Ignorant of its soulful purpose

Once a profusion of gardenias graciously offered
   Moonlight white, hypnotically fragrant
Repeatedly, betrayers ravaged her gifts
Repeatedly, deceivers trampled them underfoot
Not one paused to realize her beauty's fragility
   Assuming his own pleasure to be its purpose
Failing to appreciate the richness of her present
Failing to acknowledge his hand in her pain

Season after season precious blooms given freely
   Until thoughtless abuse ceased the budding
Angry she had not warily guarded her dowry
Angry with others' control over her plight
She failed herself, not seeing the strength within
   Submitting to the power outside, not believing
Doubting deeply, quietly agreeing, slowly losing
Doubting enough to softly step away from herself

Greenery gone, stark brittle wood remained
        Relieved when the tornado broke her free
Blindly, she spun amid debris and dirt
Blindly, she raced toward some unknown destiny
She survived the transformation, branches cracking on all sides
        Leaving her stripped smooth, her inner core
Stunned by the force of these winds of change
Stunned by the fresh raw feeling of her nakedness

Planted afresh in coarse sand awash in sunshine
        Her roots plunging deep for needed nourishment
Exhilarated by her newfound solitude
Exhilarated by the warmth of the ever-present light
The evolving texture of her new skin instilling awe
        Startling her with each new protrusion, each new bristle
Empowered by the growing protected self
Empowered by this uncultivated, wild beauty

Angles of firm flesh, seeking contentment with new form
        Disconcerted with thorny shell, an awkward protection
Admitting guardians were needed . . . for now
Admitting love was deserved . . . still wary
Soulful healing was to be absorbed indefinitely
        Until she'd grown beyond harm's reach
Hopeful then for opulent abundance in a new season
Hopeful for the touch of the caressing gardener

# The Emergence

The cocoon wrapped so tightly
    Layer upon layer
    Year after year
    Thicker, harder
    Deeper inside she was buried

Another's vision of her life shaped the past
    Action upon action
    Decision after decision
    Further, more distant
    Losing any sense of herself

Knowledge of the inner self long ago lost
    Others' needs coming first
    Others' voices louder than hers
    Others' lives taking precedence
    Her self disappearing into the depths of
        the cocoon

The cocoon took on its own beauty
    Layers of dimension
    Colors of experience
    Texture of achievement
    Outwardly attractive to many

For all the cocoon was the woman
    Pleased with the superficial talents
    Delighted by the surface personality
    Entertained by the bright smile
    Unsuspecting of anything beneath the surface

All the while she lay dormant, protected
    Her sensitivity sheltered
    Her tenderness harbored
    Her spontaneity chambered
    Her gifts safeguarded until the chosen time

Almost without warning, the cocoon cracked open
    Glimpses of brightness
    Hints of incredible beauty
    Inklings of indescribable joy
    Suggestions of greatness yet to be

Emerging from deep within, her wings unfolding
    Carefully unfurling
    Stretching full length
    Testing the flexibility
    Cautiously finding virgin flight

Fully unfolded, her beauty breathtaking
        Intricate designs unseen before
        Vivid hues enchanting the eye
        Graceful movement delighting
        Soaring, reaching new heights, new feelings

Swiftly worries and concerns land on her wings
        Weighting her flight
        Limiting her heights
        Controlling her experiences
        Threatening to end the beginning

Unwilling to relinquish her newfound freedom
        Determined to soar
        Committed to grow
        Empowered to share
        Motivated to discover her true mission

Throwing the worries and concerns from her wings
        Focusing on the new heights to be explored
        Striving to master new flight patterns
        Delighting in the higher atmospheres
        Forbidding daily demands from grounding flight

The exquisite butterfly travels the expanse of the sky
        Enrapturing all with her beauty
        Engaging all with her gifts
        Encouraging others to join her flight
        Enriching God's world with her love

*Therefore, tell them, "This is what the Sovereign LORD*
*says: No more delay! I will now do everything I have*
*threatened. I, the Sovereign LORD, have spoken!"*
**(Ezek. 12:28)**

*The Hope*

# MY JOURNEY

Disengagement from my marriage was not an easy process. I had to deal with my husband's disbelief and initial lack of comprehension of the severity of the problem. There were multiple accusations made, attempts to manipulate and control, just as in the past, but for the first time, I was beginning to understand those attempts for what they were. For the first time, I was able to step back and make a choice not to participate in this battle in which I had already been deemed the loser. In fact, in this battle there really are no winners, despite the abuser believing he is the winner. Armed with that perspective, I could avoid some of the skirmishes, but the battleground did not disappear.

We had agreed to treat each other with respect and dignity in front of our sons and our friends in order to set the tone for how others would be able to handle this difficult situation. It worked well; people did not know for months that we were even separated. We were always an excellent team in public. As co-leaders in volunteer organizations, we continued those roles in two very visible organizations for the year of our separation, as well as in our role as parents for our sons in their schools.

The journey did not get easier once he moved out, although in many respects I had a brand-new peace I never had before. Establishing boundaries was difficult, since this was still his house, too, in many respects. From a positive aspect, my sons and I had a freedom in our relationship we had not had before, and they were confiding in me with ease. However, we had to discover new ways of communicating as a total family since we were no longer all together under one roof. Information sharing was still important, and problems arose when we didn't communicate effectively. The boys were exploring how to rebuild the relationship between father and sons. Meanwhile, I negotiated the rough waters of ending a long marriage.

In the process, multiple events occurred that continued to rock my world. I kept wondering when things were going to improve. I lost my job, then had a car accident, suffering a compressed fracture of the T12 vertebrae. Finding a new job meant leaving the state, my friends, and particularly my family, including my youngest son to finish his senior year in high school living with friends of his older brother on a nearby college campus. I lost money in selling the house. My associate pastor in my home church committed suicide. One month later, the weekend I was moving everything out of my home to bring to my new home, my pastor in my home church committed suicide. I couldn't even stay for the funeral, and he was one of my closest friends. Then to cap off that nine-month period, my new employer reneged on promises made during my hiring.

All the while, however, the Lord continued to speak to me in the strongest voice, promising me that He would honor my obedience to Him in listening to His call to take this job, leave the boys to heal their relationship with their father, and for me to be healed by Him. He also promised to honor my strength in leaving the abuse and breaking the cycle for my sons. He loved me (and still does!) and knew of my love for Him and would continue to bless me in spite of all of the seemingly difficult circumstances that were befalling me at the time.

He reminded me of the rainbow He placed in the sky within an hour of the For Sale sign being pounded in the ground in front of my old house. "We have a covenant," the Lord said. I felt His love in new and wonderful ways. I never felt alone in all these difficulties. I never doubted His hand was on me, guiding me through these times. I even felt Him pick me up and carry me over ice-covered, rocky mountains and protect me from the bitter cold winds.

A month after I moved, He gave me a vision when I was readying for work one morning. The Lord showed me a large, indoor venue with several thousand people, mostly women, seated and listening to me on a stage. I was speaking to them about overcoming abuse with faith and courage, and I was holding a book in my hand. The Lord told me I had written the book. I thought, "Wow, I guess there is a reason I have gone through what I have." I thought nothing more about it at the time, but I had an incredible sense of purpose and of hope.

# PART 5

# The Fulfillment

he journey has been an amazing one—from the depths of worthlessness to reveling in God's love moment to moment. Gaining just a glimmer of understanding of the infinite depths of His love for me—*and for you*—has brought me to His feet countless times. My excitement and eagerness in serving Him and waiting to see what He wants to do with this life with which He has blessed me brightens each day.

If you are still struggling with abuse, let me assure you that this same joy can also be yours. I struggled for so many years that I don't need to count them. The power in them, however, is the woman I am today *because of those struggles*.

Even though I ended my marriage, my faith has been extraordinarily tested in the past five years of my life. Yet *because of the abuse, I had strength that did not waiver* to overcome every trial and test that I faced.

Our loving Lord has given me incredible people in my life who have lifted me and supported me throughout these last several years as I finally emerged from abuse's hold on me.

*Please trust Him; He will do the same for you!*

# Experiencing God

The intensity of experiencing God's creation
Every sense is so sharp that it is almost painful
Exquisite beauty in every star in the heavens, every leaf on a tree, every blossom on a stem
Overcome, overwhelmed, so saddened by the blindness of those around me

How can they not see how incredible a moonlit night is?
How can they not see that each star holds a promise?
How can they not sense God's hand upon them at this very moment?
How can they be so preoccupied with man's things that they miss God's things?

Gazing at the moon, I absorb the magnificence of God
Searching for each sparkling star, I see the infinity of God
Listening to the insects call, I understand the tenderness of God
Feeling the slight breeze, I feel the very breath of God

Each nerve ending of my being is awakened
Every sound, every sight, every sensation reminds me of
      His awesomeness
Perched on the pinnacle of awareness, I catch my breath
For if I am still enough, I will see the face of God

# A Pilgrimage

A full life and yet
> A sense that there is more

A content existence and yet
> An undefined need not surfaced

Knowledge of well-being and yet
> Intuition of blessings yet to come

Speak to me, Lord, tell me what to do.

A growing awareness of the world outside my view
> Beyond the horizon escaping my eyes

A peaking eagerness to learn of the unseen
> To explore those unknown vistas

An aching in my heart for the love yet to give
> For the gifts yet to receive

Speak to me, Lord, am I heading in Your direction?

A yearning for fulfillment of unknown desires
> Yet to be felt, yet to be recognized

A searching for unused talents buried deep within
> Lying dormant, waiting to be awakened

A longing for clear focus, determined purpose
> Still distant and out of sight

Speak to me, Lord, are You sure it is me You want?

Dawn with rays of wisdom spreading upward
> Shedding early morning light of understanding

Warmth from the rising sun of recognition
> Lighting the path with purpose

Inner peace consuming all doubt of direction
> As talents are awakened by grace

Yes, Lord, I am listening . . . .

*Trust Me and I will show you the way*
*In My time and according to My plan*
*Your gifts will blossom*
*Your mission will be clear*
*You will serve Me in ways unknown to you*
*With My children whom you have not met*
*Your vision will be focused, your talents perfected*
*You will reflect far and wide My love and My grace*

Yes, Lord, I am the one You want!

# Soul Mates

Somewhere you exist
       Beyond my imagination, my dreams
I feel the power of your presence
       Pulsating, breathing, halo'ing my world
Somewhere you are waiting

Someday our paths will merge
       Unexpectedly yet effortlessly
We will know without question
       Intuitively drawn one to the other
Someday we will connect

Somehow our souls will converse
       With compassion, gentleness, patience
Eyes lock and comprehension flows
       Rusted gates and ancient walls crumble
Somehow we will trust

Somebody becomes a reality
       Without fear, reaching across the chasm of doubt
We will love unconditionally, sweetly
       Acceptance of the past without judgment
For your and my somebodys are soul mates

# The Union

A prism in a room of draped windows
    Exquisitely cut crystal, polished smooth
    Its potential for color untapped
    Lifeless, an inanimate object of beauty

The bright light illuminating all in its path
    Showing the way for those lost
    Warming the air for those chilled
    But always, just brilliant white light

Separately they served, enriching others' lives
    Individually, each was acclaimed
    Apart they existed, fulfilling expectations
    Unaware of a different path, content with this one

One day, an accidental brush of the drape
    A ray of light briefly catching the prism
    A glimmer of color momentarily appearing
    Catching the eye, hinting of hidden treasures

The flash of multiple hues, brief but intense
    Realization of untapped potential subtly dawning

Suggestion of a soulful connection, perhaps
    Birth of an unsought, but miraculous union, maybe

More deliberately, drapes drawn back for a moment
    Steady stream of light directed
    Hungrily absorbed, then refracted
    A delicate arch of pastel painted

The realm of possibilities now exposed
    Rich blessings of a union perceived
    Tantalizing what-ifs now considered
    Dreams yet to be dreamed breathe life

With unbridled excitement drapes anchored open
    With heightened anticipation, bright light pours out
    An infinite spectrum of color bursts forth
    Observers dazzled by the richness and depth

The connection of two souls welded forever
    Rainbows twinkling in every direction
    Completion of each through their union
    Blessing all whose gaze falls upon them

# The Key

The key's click reverberated through my soul
       Echoing in the empty caverns of my life
The last tumbler of the lock fell into place
       Breaking decades' hold on this chest
Lid lifts away, magically, effortlessly
       Releasing the sides of the heavy box

The treasure within illuminated after ages of darkness
       Recognizing nothing at first, so strange
The revelation so unexpected, so sudden
       Catching me unaware, off guard
The brilliance yet purity of the jewel
       Stunning me, leaving me awestruck

Mesmerized, frozen in time, sat I
       Holding my heart in my hands
Realization dawns, in all its complexities
       Unlayering multi-dimensions of glorious color
With each layer unveiled, greater depths respond
       Driving electric currents stronger into my soul

Without expectation, without fear, eyes wide open
       Letting go of past hurts and scars
Gingerly, I cradle this precious new gem in my grasp
       Examining it from every angle, exploring
Amazed at its clarity, its unquestioned definition
       Acknowledging its uniqueness in this world

This is mine, yet it is not
       Giving and receiving freely means no ownership
Still, remarkably, the deepest, most resilient bond ever
       Connecting me to you in the supernatural
My soul touches yours outside space and time
       Speaking in unmarred, unselfish agape love

I love and am loved, so honestly, so purely
       Wanting nothing from you, nor you from me
Each other's peace and joy, our hearts' desire
       Filling those soulful moments of contemplation
No sacrifice too great, no prayer too small
       Entreating for a life trouble free and purposeful

You, the key God used that memorable moment

      Unlocking my heart after decades of darkness

You, gentle, caring, trustworthy teacher

      Sharing God's gift of pure love, requiring nothing

You, the arms of God, angel, and shepherd

      Guiding me into self-acceptance and love


Time will pass inevitably as do events

      Changing the world around us

Eternally entwined we will remain throughout

      Sharing a spiritual dimension few ever know

However the future shapes our meeting and speaking

      Remaining forever with me are you, my Key.

*But those who trust in the LORD will find new strength. They will soar high on wings like eagles. They will run and not grow weary. They will walk and not faint.*
**(Isa. 40:31)**

# The Fulfillment

## MY JOURNEY

aiting upon the Lord and living with the belief that His strength renewed me daily was often all that sustained me. I walked truly by faith alone, because I did not have a clue what my future held. I knew the pain of the past and the present were often overwhelming, yet somehow deep within me, I also unquestionably knew that my Lord was holding me in His arms.

The intimacy of my relationship with Him was growing at such an accelerated pace that I marveled at His revelations to me. I would kneel at my bedside and feel Him take my head into His lap, stroke my hair, and assure me that this was all temporary. I could feel His love wash over me in such a powerful way that sometimes His presence was real. My hand would grow hot as He held it

My Lord knew how lonely it was for me without my sons and my friends. He knew how exhausted and frustrated I was in my job. He knew His plans for me and He had His timing. Within seven months of my relocating, and only two months after the suicides of my pastor and associate pastor in my home church in North Carolina, and the selling of my old home, He specifically directed me to a new church home via a direct message to my former next-door neighbor, Kelly Matthews, to whom I will be forever indebted. Fortunately, she is an obedient servant and wrote to me immediately, directing me to the church and pastor.

Trinity Chapel was thirty-five miles away—a Church of God. I had never been to a Church of God in my life, but I knew the Holy Spirit's voice when He spoke, and I obeyed immediately.

The first Sunday I attended, the guest speaker was an archbishop from a Syrian Orthodox church who kept my riveted attention for two and a half hours. Every part of his message was directed to my life. I returned the next Sunday and heard Pastor, now Bishop, Jim Bolin speak and have the very same impact on me. When I went to a business meeting of the church the following Thursday, upon the instruction of Holy Spirit once again, I realized I was there for two reasons. The first was to open the church's eyes to the needs of people with significant disabilities, my field at the time. But the second reason was the Holy Spirit's message for me. Bishop Bolin announced the acceleration of the expansion program of the sanctuary and displayed the architect's renderings of the interior of the new sanctuary. That scene, populated with a crowd, was the same vision I had been given the previous summer in which I had been speaking to people about overcoming abuse. I realized that I was beginning to enter a new phase of my life, in which the Lord would be fulfilling the purposes for which He created me.

Our struggles do not end simply because we have overcome abuse in our lives. The vulnerabilities that were within me still linger in the corners of my being and will surface in times of stress, disappointment, or loneliness. However, I have learned such valuable lessons about combating them. I know most importantly that God loves me abundantly, and when I am at my lowest, I retreat into the throne room with Him and seek His love. I let Him love me back into wholeness, knowing no human being can do that for me. I curl up on my bed and ask Him to hold me and He does. Peace returns to my heart and the tears stop flowing. I have the strength to face the next hurdle and the next day. I am more capable of *agape* love than ever before. I know how to love unselfishly because that is how He loves me. I can love freely because He has freed me.

I pray that I may somehow assist you in finding that same love and freedom in Him. And most important, I pray that you will grasp that no man, no woman, no human being on this earth will fill the void you have in your heart. Only God can fill your need for love. His perfect love is that which you seek. Submit yourself to Him and seek Him to fill you with the gift of love He has to offer you. Then and only then will you have the peace you so desperately seek. Then and only then will you be able to give and receive the kind of love you not only desire, but deserve.

*Whom have I in heaven but you?*
*I desire you more than anything on earth.*
*My health may fail and my spirit may grow weak,*
*but God remains the strength of my heart;*
*he is mine forever.*
**(Ps. 73:25–26)**

# Beginning Your Journey with Jesus Christ

You have lived my journey with me and experienced how powerful my relationship with the Lord was and still is. I would not have survived without Him. Where are you? If you have this book in your hands, you have most likely experienced some aspect of abuse in your life, whether you are a victim, friend or family member of a victim, or perhaps an abuser trying desperately to turn around. No matter what your circumstance, change begins at the foot of the cross. Paul stated in Philippians 4:13, "I can do everything through Christ, who gives me strength." If you have accepted Christ as your Savior and you have truly turned your life over to Him, you are, through Him, capable of changing every aspect of your life. You may have long ago as a child or an adolescent professed your acceptance of Jesus as your Savior—not truly understanding the significance of that decision—and then not truly walking in it. No matter what is in your past, today is fresh and new. The beauty of our Savior's love and His sacrifice is that He gives us all an opportunity to become new creatures in Him. Paul also wrote in Ephesians 2:10, "For we are God's masterpiece. He has created us anew in Christ Jesus, so we can do the good things he planned for us long ago."

Whether you need to renew your commitment or make a commitment for the first time, accepting Jesus as your Savior is not complicated. We begin with the simple concept that there is a separation between God and humanity; that separation is caused by sin. In Romans 3:23, Paul stated it very simply: "For everyone has sinned; we all fall short of God's glorious standard." A sinner cannot enter into God's presence; therefore entrance into the heavenly kingdom is not possible as long as we are in a sinful state. Acceptance of this fact must precede our desire for salvation; otherwise the need for a savior does not exist.

Next we must acknowledge that God provided the only acceptable bridge across the chasm that separated us from Him. Jesus Christ, perfectly sinless as God and yet born as a man from a virgin, died as the perfect sacrifice to take the burden of our sins so that we could be presented pure and sinless to God and enter into His presence to spend eternity with Him. John 3:16 says, "For God loved the world so much that he gave his one and only Son, so that everyone who believes in him will not perish but have eternal life." It is God's desire that everyone come into eternal life, but the only way is through belief in His Son. Jesus Himself said in John 14:6, "I am the way, the truth, and the life. No one can come to the Father except through me."

Critical to this step is your understanding that Jesus' act of sacrifice was personal; He did this for you. If you had been the only person on the face of the earth, He still would have died for you. He whispered your name as He said from the cross, "Father, forgive them, for they don't know what they are doing" (Luke 23:34). Our sins, all of our sins, were forgiven that afternoon as He died on that cross, but we must ask for and then accept His forgiveness. Without Jesus' sacrifice we were doomed—there is no other way. If you don't meet Jesus face to face at the cross and *believe* this was for you, personally and individually, a personal relationship with Him will be impossible.

But wait; there is another very important step in this process. It is not enough to simply ask God to forgive us and accept the sacrifice Jesus made on our behalf. We must repent to God for the sins of our life. In other words, we must turn from our old way of life and commit to following a different course. In Acts 17:30, Paul gave the Athenians a message that is as pertinent today as it was then: "Now he commands everyone everywhere to repent of their sins and turn to him." When we accept Jesus Christ as our Savior, we begin the process of changing our mind and our heart to emulate our newly reborn spirit. This makes it difficult to follow the habits of old, the sinful ways that once were customary for us. Repentance means a change of mind, and change is transformation.

In Titus 3:5-6, Paul wrote, "He saved us, not because of the righteous things we had done, but because of His mercy. He washed away our sins, giving us a new birth and a new life through the Holy Spirit. He generously poured out the Spirit upon us through Jesus Christ our Savior."

It is through God's grace and the regenerating power of His Holy Spirit that we are transformed and become new creations in Christ. In Galatians 6:15, Paul stated, "What counts is whether we have been transformed into a new creation." Please understand that from His Holy Spirit you will receive the strength, the power, and the ongoing grace to heal, to overcome, to become the whole beautiful person God intended you to be from the beginning of time.

We must continue to walk with Him, no matter what circumstances may confront us as we move away from abuse and, in His grace, into a life free from abuse. There will be trials and tribulations, no doubt, but be encouraged by the apostle Peter's words: "So be truly glad. There is wonderful joy ahead, even though you have to endure many trials for a little while" (1 Pet. 1:6). God has such awesome plans for you. All He asks is that you trust and follow Him. Jeremiah 29:11–14 is a wonderful promise:

> "For I know the plans I have for you," says the LORD. "They are plans for good and not for disaster, to give you a future and a hope. In those days when you pray, I will listen. If you look for me wholeheartedly, you will find me. I will be found by you," says the LORD. "I will end your captivity and restore your fortunes. I will gather you out of the nations where I sent you and will bring you home again to your own land."

# *Coming Next!*

## THOSE WHO ARE CALLED

by Janice Clark Hayes

At some point in our lives, we heard a faint voice whisper into our souls and thought perhaps it was the voice of God. A few amazing individuals listened and responded immediately. We know some of them, either personally or by their impact. But for the vast majority of us, it took years. Travel with the author as she explores journeys along that rocky road from the first whisper to understanding what Romans 8:28 truly means: "And we know that God causes everything to work together for the good of those who love God and are called according to his purpose for them."

To find out more information
visit us at:
www.journeyofaconqueror.com

You can contact Janice at:
Janice@journeyofaconqueror.com

To order additional copies of this title call:
1-877-421-READ (7323)
or please visit our Web site at
www.winepressbooks.com

If you enjoyed this quality custom-published book,
drop by our Web site for more books and information.

www.winepressgroup.com
"Your partner in custom publishing."